The Phoenix Living Poets

POEMS FROM ITALY

Poets Published in
The Phoenix Living Poets Series

★

ALEXANDER BAIRD · ALAN BOLD

GEORGE MACKAY BROWN

JENNIFER COUROUCLI

GLORIA EVANS DAVIES

PATRIC DICKINSON · D. J. ENRIGHT

JOHN FULLER · DAVID GILL

J. C. HALL · MOLLY HOLDEN

JOHN HORDER · P. J. KAVANAGH

RICHARD KELL · LAURIE LEE

LAURENCE LERNER

CHRISTOPHER LEVENSON

EDWARD LOWBURY · NORMAN MACCAIG

JAMES MERRILL · RUTH MILLER

LESLIE NORRIS · ROBERT PACK

ARNOLD RATTENBURY

ADRIENNE RICH · JON SILKIN

JON STALLWORTHY

GILLIAN STONEHAM

EDWARD STOREY · TERENCE TILLER

SYDNEY TREMAYNE

LOTTE ZURNDORFER

POEMS
FROM ITALY

by

R. H. BOWDEN

CHATTO AND WINDUS

THE HOGARTH PRESS

1970

Published by
Chatto and Windus Ltd
with The Hogarth Press Ltd
42 William IV Street
London WC 2

★

Clarke, Irwin and Co Ltd
Toronto

Distributed in the United States of America
by Wesleyan University Press

ISBN: 0 8195 7029 X

Printed in Great Britain

To Riki

Contents

To Italy at Fifty

I

Newhaven-Dieppe

Inside the salt-rimmed ship a crush of school-children
suck straws, spit pips,
carrying their curiosity and garbage to another shore.
Above dark anoraks lank hair co-mingles
with the smell of hard-boiled eggs and Channel fog.
Along the slanting decks crushed cigarettes like slugs
slide to the blurred grey waves.
The voices slur, the engines mumble,
thoughts criss-cross like wire
abrasive on the air's damp skin,
or lie and stare punch-drunk
with adolescent melancholy at unravelled clouds.
Beyond the rail slack seas shake and revoke
each last connection with faint families.

II

Urbino: Madonna by Piero della Francesca

In grey disguise
her slant hieratic eyes
gaze out at us untroubled by our want.
Their hard serene
composure shares a diamond world
where light is knowing;
pure median to the pendulum swing of time
her heart stands still. This child
is not from her, but plucked from life displays

stigmata printed in another world, another time, where pain
inscribes its record purely at pure surfaces. Our pain
is not skin-deep; it pierces time, invades it to the quick:
yet her calm eyes, her brows, that child's still face,
stare down towards us so coldly immortal
that our nightmares cease.

III

In Italy at Fifty

Has age turned me to bone?
A hint of marble masks the once-soft sky;
birds' voices scrape like chalk,
once urgent leaves fork stick-like,
dead grass blunts the air:
the soil hides ashes' tongues,
blood's fire is rare across this landscape
once flamed with tulip's scarlet, strung with fireflies' wire,
and purpled to the heart with throb of nightingales.
Buds flake with rust: a snail-shell,
grey and gold like wax,
pours out the grey dust of an empty spring.
Whole valleys whiten as the light grows dim:
tomorrow's thunder bunches up its limbs
and prowls along the horizon like an antique lion.

IV

Easter Eve, Urbino: Dreams, Bells, Hailstones

That night I lay relaxed,
a body waiting for a mould to grow into.
Outside, the Duomo and the rooftops gleamed like shells:
the sky, a sea of carbon, ebbed and flowed between
the campanile and the outline of my room.

I slept:
the blackness gathered into me, filled out my dreams.
Each quarter-hour
the clock on the Duomo struck sleep's death:
my dreams swooped round the campanile like scared birds.
I turned and slept again:
the carbon in the sky was turned to stone,
the hail had turned the roofs to sugared bread.
Night drank me to the bone:
again the awakening bells
laid out new dreams like dice along the window-sill.
Then thunder came; a black hand gloved and soft
began to rattle on the window-pane.

I roused, sat up: the dice fell from the sill:
the moonlight glistened in a scarf of silk.
I held my hands like prisoners in the hollow light.
The dreams sang round me: "Christ is reborn again."
"Again? Again?" – The dreams began to laugh.
The hail marched down the street like lines of broken spears.
"Christ is reborn . . ." A dream,
thrust like a rocket, burst inside my head.
Its white incendiary flowers flew through my eyes:
a gust of ashen hail
veered through my fingers on the window-sill.

All round, the palace shutters groaned on rusted hasps:
the wind blew out the carbon from the sky;
the cold bells ran like lizards towards the morning sun.
The pavements far below, still ashen grey,
creaked with black crumbs of charcoal as my thoughts uncurled
and climbed to the day's horizon on rinsing steps of glass.

V

Talking to Leopardi

So there it is: I've come back again in the spring.
Perhaps, after all, if you too could only come back
you would find it all still the same.
– Or are things different now? Here, after the shower,
there's the smell of damp wood-ash rising
swung to and fro by the bees;
while down there
                    a white petal falls
clinging, as you remember,
                    to the dampness of scarcely formed leaves.
And above, on the hillside,
                    do you remember
how under the tight green nipples of figs,
the upturned share of a plough
seems to cut the blue soil of the sky
that glides so tranquilly past it?
Earth, sky and flower:
                    are these all still the same?
Yes: "Fango, fango è il mondo!"
Wasn't that how you once expressed it?
All happiness is only a temporary release from sorrow,
all life only brief emergence from mud.
We return
          to mud.
Into mud,
          into sorrow
everything inevitably returns.
Well, what of it, Giacomo?
You died,
but in spite of all that you said you, too,
tried to hold back the world with your words.
That world out there? –
Yet it still goes on existing, over and over again;

every spring
        re-establishing itself far more surely
than the surest poem,
        – if only you were here still to see it.
Perhaps, then, it's we
that are the ephemeral half.
That world out there, this world is here:
why must we spend a life-time trying to immortalise *that*?
Trying to absorb it into the dark throat of ourselves,
to revive it over and over again in our dark incantations of words,
when it's we ourselves that must always remain briefly mortal?
Look, though we suck down these images of an exuberant spring
time and time again into our innermost selves
and embalm their pure essence in words,
can they ever return in an image as pure as themselves,
or rise as stringent and fresh
as the smell of this black wood-ash
        that pauses between the white cherry-flowers
to announce itself once again
        to our standing audience of nerves?
Look, however we try, we can never precisely reflect
the true essence of each thing that lies out there.
All that's purely beyond us all: it can live
more nearly immortal than we ever can. It lies sunk
in the deep bed of time, while we glide along on time's surface.
Where, then, are we all of us going?
Must we begin, from now on, to leave everything,
everything that we most loved, must we leave it
right over there beyond the far edge of our words?
This time, for instance, the spring and I,
we must both go our different ways.
That's it, Spring!
This time I'll leave you to survive
without the touch of my words
to blur or diminish your strength.

So, – there you are, Giacomo,
See how you and I were deceived!
It's you who have died, and I who must die
surviving on in the grave
anonymity of this wholly physical world. –
So, from now on,
for me, and perhaps for all that come after,
it's our silence, only, that answers the greater questions.

VI

In the Umbrian Mountains above Gubbio

Huge flanks
of an antique world festooned with cloud:
strong bones
that bore Giotto up to leave their imprint in his hand,
each time he drew a human shape implanting
memories of rock in bone,
of sky in breath, of haunched
and ribbed and pubic folds of landscape
into conjugated forms that stare
precisely at us through their planes of marble air:
brown antique world that bore Giotto up,
hold under us today still carving
a steadiness in our time,
shored light to move into,
cool held perspectives to deflect false winds,
strict distances receding to return
precise yet limitless, your contours lying becalmed
beyond the edge of this and every time!

Giotto, here
I stand beside you by the harbour of your work,
still looking through
translucent water to where
your sky floats veiled with mist
against the nipples and the pelvic ridges
that your fingers loved to trace
upon damp plaster hardening on a wall.
Up here, lying on these mountains,
your memory slides in mine;
the clear bones of your skull
move through my mouth like glass until
these words strain out to build
a human landscape as your hands once did.

Remain, Giotto, now
pure bone inside the flesh of our limp sight,
a rigid armature to mould the body of our future to.
For us, trapped in the nightmare of today,
beyond the frescoes of your mountains
great rocks and clouds roll down.
We know that twenty years ago
huge gales and tempests photographed our world:
the trembling image of our lives
was plotted out in black.
We burnt our awful frescoes on another harbour wall.
Ours cannot be forgotten, – yours perhaps survived, –
unless our crazy imprint blacks both past and future out;
then only the cold precision of these hills will stay,
bleached like a lunar negative beneath a burnt-out sky,
conveying what you saw as human to no human eyes.

VII

Spring Thunder

So green and yet so black,
the stumbling clouds knock down the buds of spring:
the lightning scatters needles in the plain.
Scented with bean-flowers, rinsed with distant showers,
the wind picks at the hillside:
outriders of the storm
fall flat as pebbles on the matted straw.
A grey
haze off the mountain
drifts relentlessly across. Cold grease
fills up the eyes and blocks the nose,
as contadini under sacking,
knees nailed like trees with rain,
clamber towards their houses,
feet lamed by spring's ripe clay.

VIII

Boy Herding Pigs

How lovely to lie
hidden in long warm grass
like a succulent, odorous
chlorophyll skin of oneself,
white flowers at one naked shoulder,
watching the pig's fat sighs;
then relaxing, closing the eyes
into odoriferous splendour,
floating on seas
of bean-flower,
warm green corn and damp vetch,
until suddenly,
opening an eye again, one confronts
the pig, –

like a god,
malevolent,
his red-rimmed eye
a-bristle with stiff gold lashes
staring
impersonally.
One grunt:
then the pig's hot breath,
straight from his earth-lined bowels,
bursts over the boy.
Look, how the sun shines through
those ears!
Straight through!
All sky,
pale pink!
And the head advancing
onto him,
into him.

One more snort,
one great burst of breath
as though from the bowels of the earth,
and the reins of the pigs saliva have harnessed him powerless,
holding him up
for the last immaculate squeal . . .

But then, at the crucial moment,
a bee swings, drunk from the scent of the beans,
through the pig's opened mouth.
One sputter,
one gasp for breath as his head sways up,
and the pale pink sky swings down,
all blue, torn to shreds;
nothing left.
Just a swift pulsation of heart-beats
and a squeal driven into the ground.

PFI—B

IX

How to kill an Italian Landscape

So pure
that even air moves through
these colours trapped in glass
beyond the mirror of my consciousness:
and only I opaque,
blocking the sunlight with interior views
of blackened years,
unfolding portraits, masks of yesterday.

So thin,
the senses scarcely grasp
these colours trembling in a lake,
these skies like apertures,
these forms like breath
pressed on a window-pane.

So faintly touched with permanence
that I stand by,
a photograph blocked in black and white
that wills
such frail impermanence to set,
a setting for myself,
a two-way landscape that can fit no camera's outward eye.

And yet
this inner-outer image I still long to fix,
to haul out later in some drawing-room,
then hand it round from eye to other eye,
each blocked up with its own interior monologue of lies.

So false
this image trapped inside these lines:
see how it lies,
all touch of first impermanence removed,
quite dulled, remote, congealed,
till thrust aside some day and locked up in a drawer,
just like myself it fades back on the page,
all light denied, a bruise
that simply goes right out of sight;
its final end concealed
discretely in a narrow box of words.

X

Graffiti at Petriolo

Somewhere
on the other side of my mind
a bomb explodes under a hotel,
a Buddhist burns in a Saigon square.
Who cares?
Distantly
such suffering matters,
makes some sense.
Calamities
are scribbled down,
whole wallfuls of their grey graffiti
scratched, as though with childish hands,
upon the further side of my worn brain.

And yet this side
a nightingale still sings,
a lizard crawls,
a dog barks by a water-trough;
beyond the hill
the streets of Petriolo fall asleep.

I cross the hill:
just there
on Petriolo's broken walls
are other words,
another language
takes the world apart, and coughs,
and puts it down
on walls that crumble from a war that passed on twenty years ago.

I stand and read: "VIVA IL DUCE!"

and here, superimposed: "FUORI CANI AMERICANI,"
                                          "PACE IN VIETNAM."
An ant crawls through my fingers,
between my feet a lizard falls.
Through other fingers ants crawl slowly down:
those fingers once made scratches on some wall.
Bright lizards now run through their arteries searching for their
                                                        brain.

I turn and walk away . . .

That war inside takes place two continents away:
this war I fight today
breaks down closed walls of sunlight,
searches through their ruins
for some new fragment that will light a line.
"In Saigon flames ascend like screaming flights of birds."
Does my war matter? Wandering on confused,
I scribble grey graffiti in a cul-de-sac of brain.

White Cockerel

Perched in ruined dignity upon the trademans' van,
white feathers clipped and frayed to prevent escape,
he lifts a yellow foot, then stands there poised,
unconscious of the end that's soon to come.

Now leaning in the wind, his feathers rippling
in a frippery of curls that close his eyes,
he shuffles sideways, stiffens, clips his dragon claws
on to a crate where blowsy hens still doze.

The van moves on, the cockerel staggers back:
his pricked eyes blink as scales chink in the wind.
A crate above his head is torn aside:
extracted by her legs, a hen hangs upside-down.

With wings entangled in the tradesman's hands,
she jolts the pointer on the scales now up, now down.
The cockerel stares beyond the tradesman's head
to see above black rooftops pigeons drift and glow.

The hen goes down the street held upside-down:
the cockerel, lifting on his heels, attempts to fly;
inflates his body full, then blinks and blinks again,
while strong convulsions gulp him full of sun.

With round breast rising, head held back, he crows, and crows
and crows.

What life goes out cannot come back again.
No knife shall ever find it when his feathers fall,
nor nerve reshape it when his neck is wrung.

In Italy: Neither Here Nor There

Ascoli: the Duomo in Rain

Black rain on the black shawls of the women
and in the church twilight,
a thick darkness thrust in by leather doors;
only the windows tearful, their eyelids moth-grey, patterned
                                                    like petals,
and the gold scimitars over the altar cut like Crivelli's crowns.
Yet the people stand there in blackness,
a blank preying blackness under their great straddled god
whose legs are walls to the rain, whose groin
stretched glistening over their heads
rings out with the sound of brilliant chrysalid voices
bursting from shells of black rain.
Till the echoes beat like a swarm, then slowly
cease to vibrate, as the black
people
            bow
                    down,
under the tower of their god,
where they kneel carved
to a stone husk of silence, three-quarters immersed in past time:
while we,
visitors from another city, another country,
thumb our way out through the rain,
going inevitably nowhere,
afloat on a negligent river
that drifts us remorselessly on.

Words

The words
form themselves into blots
under the landscape,

pressing forward to turn into "rock,"
into "tree," "lake," "farm," "sky," "cloud,"
till the screen of the landscape itself
lies broken, blotted out with black words.
Then the mountains fall
thin as wafers, the sky
powders off with the wind,
and the colours
fade into varnish clogging the cracks of the mind.
Oh, far better some day if the landscape itself should climb
sponging out blots of strung words,
till it lies,
coiled and curled,
smoothed with my five senses' fingers
over the word-dead, thought-lost contours of the at last
immaculate brain.

Ascoli: White Flowers by the Amphitheatre

The flowers send down the evening street
a thin perfume of whiteness.
It spreads out
beyond the Caltex sign to where
the stones of the Roman amphitheatre smoulder in dark grass.
It envelops above
those four nuns who, white-breasted like birds,
float down a long flight of steps to the town.
Out there,
in the moth-flustered twilight it moves
where the girls pass and repass, their flickering hands
caught in a cobweb of words, their laughter
tossed in the gutters like breaking fragments of glass.
It fades out
somewhere remotely up there on the darkening hillside,

where the cars purr off into silence
stringing bright lights up the Apennines,
nosing their way towards Rome.
But down here it stays,
trapped by the damp stones of villas,
nudging and edging the blackness,
choking the stamens of flowers whose petals fall
like long white togas urging up night from the ground.

On the Way to Montelupone

Two lizards sleep on the lip of a hollow tree,
yellow-green like two strands of dried moss.
Then one moves, wriggles on
clipped by its black wire toes to the side of the tree:
a small pulse throbs under one arm-pit,
its heart knocks on the grey bark.
The sun grows warmer, the lizard's belly swells and extends,
its fingers fidget, it turns
to a new landscape of bark.
It runs down, belly accepting the trunk, to the ground,
then comes back.
Its mate turns a disinterested head;
a black ant dawdles along.
No conversation,
only a common acceptance of the same creased trunk of a tree.
And the ant travels downwards
into the black land of last autumn's leaves.

Corridonia

So there we sat in the huge billiard saloon,
while outside the rain and thunder came down
on the blue-green rows of hills and the trembling cities.
The billiard-balls clicked, white on green;

the red-white-and-blue ceiling vibrated with stereo-music;
the boys sprawled strong-legged like frogs
or rolled each other on the marble floor.
We sat in the billiard saloon and drank martinis.
The rain came down and the crude abstract paintings
blurted from the wall formless, meaningless questions that no
one answered.
Below, in the public gardens, the silly sculpture
squirted and squatted, opened in wide pubic gestures
on to the long undulations of Sybilline hills.
Back and forth the music swung, echoing the prodigality of all
existence,
whistling, belching, farting, asking . . .
Oh, God knows what? Who cares how?
shouting its endless chain of meaningless questions
over the solemn ranges of rain-drenched hills.

Then the music stopped.
We still sat on,
and the rain came endlessly down
till the mountains swam on the windows like strong black wine.

Walking on the Tuscan Hills

(i)

Listen, we cannot retain it now; for whatever we do
the stiff cruel fingers of the past draw everything down into
deeper darkness.
Only, from time to time, entirely by accident
a shape remains caught in a word,
the sound of a bell
rocks in the future over a distant stream.

Thus Michaelangelo, growing older,
found everything past was beyond redeeming,
everything was lost in the growing rock.
For him, far more than for us, time was not clear.
There were no "open sesames" left to him.
The windows, that had once opened out of his life,
had grown, now, more and more infrequent.
So that in the end, staring out from that last high tower
and finding that everywhere around him the air had become rock,
he fell face forward,
enclosed but never falling, in that boundless rock of time,
sealed
       in a sculptural purgatory where slaves,
like Tuscan mountains, wrestled with the receding light.

(ii)

Climbing out of the mist, the Tuscan hills,
blue with the last day's rain,
bristle black into sunlight.
The seed of a bird falls
into the open mouth of the sky.
Rivers-distant the Arno wakes up another vein.
Under trees, a hand's breadth away,
celandine flicker, anemones stretch
in their first violent lilac,
skinned to the sensitive vein. Under the last year's oaks
the young pigs sweat and grovel.
Time swings
         thistle and muscle,
bristle and lover,
         into a smoother groove.

Under the cypresses the derelict graves,
surrounded by the refuse of the picnickers,
throw back warm sunlight.
What holds the dead from us
is only crumbling stones, a broken wall,
and the bright, unlived hypocrisy of plastic flowers.

Poems from Italy

XIII QUADRI

(Collected between Macerata and Montelupone)

I: La Nonna

In the garden of pale peonies
parting the petals of flowers
with the tip of a lame stick,
the old woman inserts the sun
minute by minute into the growing flower.
Beneath her black head-scarf the folds of her forehead clench
tightly,

biting off one by one the petals of
too bright a spring.

II: Infants' School

Rolling each other like balls of grass
over and over again and again in the hot sunlight,
perched on railings, picking at noses,
or, like sparrows, pecking up dirt,
or, relaxed on the ground, scribbling sensations caught first
at the tips of young fingers,
the children burrow ways into each other's eyes and ears,
throw dust at the bland face of the sky, –
then fall asleep
in the waves of chlorophylled air
that rise from the fresh, sweating plants
crushed below between streams
and the white fondling fists of the sun.

III: *The Water Pump*

Taking the blue water-pump on the tractor,
driving it high up the grazed groin of the valley,
the contadino follows spring,
lifts it a little higher
with the slim jet pumped from the nozzle.
For a moment the heat retreats,
soil opens: but over the crest of the hill
three men, hoeing up the light brown crust,
faces turned to blackness under their wide-brimmed hats,
pause and look down. On the road below
the silver bristles of a dead hedgehog scatter
under the wheels of a cart, while high above
the silver jets still bounce and shake off the sun.

IV: *Scuola Femminile*

The little girls,
black pigtails jumping off white-smocked shoulders,
pause to watch the two men,
glistening with sweat on hairs of arms and chests,
fixing with twin pliers
the wire fence round the school enclosure.

Beyond the fence a hunched, wirey rat
disappears into the loose, young corn.

V: *Insects*

The blue-bottles, feeding on the crushed belly of the hedgehog,
rise and fly off amongst the heavy-burdened flowers.
Black midges and gnats cast specks of shadow
on to the white dust of road.

The hum of a bee
disappears behind my left ear
into the unknown hillside.
A black beetle crawls four-square in the blinding sun
going (determinedly) nowhere.

VI: Mezzogiorno

Contadino in blue shirt and wide-brimmed hat
returns from freshly tied vines across the cornfield,
in one hand empty water-bottle and hoe,
in the other sandals.
Between the corn his two mild animal feet
mould to the ground,
while the white of the clouds, the blue of the distant mountains,
shine through the glass of his empty water-bottle.

Seated, still tying vines on the slant skyline,
an old man with a crushed felt hat
picks at a broken tooth.
The sky shows through his open mouth.

VII: Noises

In the middle of a wide valley I lost my way:
the path disappeared into green corn.
The peasants for miles around, working in the fields,
paused and stared down at me.
By a distant house a dog barked, a boy shouted.
Above on the hillside nightingales and larks were shouting
                                                    directions.
The wind blew suddenly up the hillside, through the bare twigs
                                        of young fig-trees,
rustling the corn-blades.

A lizard stood still, scraped its legs, then disappeared through a
                                        crack in the ground.
As I didn't know where I was going, or what was the name
                                        of the town,
(if there was one,)
it was no use asking the way.
Then a Lambretta appeared on the distant skyline,
going from somewhere to somewhere.
The wind blew coolly from east to west.
I sat on, on the open hillside,
till the noises dried up in the sun.

VIII: The Stream

The poplars hold up their leaves
like small bronze plates to the sky.
The water trickles past grey trunks:
a brimstone butterfly wanders vaguely between nettles and
                                        purple bugle.
The stream burrows and rambles between the dead brambles
                        and briars of the recent winter,
its waters so full of soil that no sky shows.
When a plane shoots silver overhead,
its shadow disturbs no reflection;
only the shiney bronze plates of the poplars
are dulled as though by a slim finger
that touches momentarily
and immediately is removed from them.

IX: Blue Lambretta

His shirt ballooning behind him deep blue in the breeze,
he climbs
past houses colour-washed pale blue,
to pause

to exchange three words only
with the driver of the minibus, dully blue;
then rides, past green hedges,
to disappear over the bright skyline,
blue lost in blue;
only the two metal wheels shining through dust,
dust falling to blue behind him.

X: *Montelupone*

This is a town that has been left on one side.
Today, the walls of the basilica
are cracked by weather from vault to foundation.
A huge terra-cotta urn, twice the size of a man,
lurches sideways before the altar,
standing precariously upside-down
as though dropped disconsolately from the lap of the gods.
To the north, the war memorial gardens
are filled with rubble and rusted ironwork.
Children play there with dolls on the rankly overgrown steps;
yet the willow-trees are pruned
and the neat pollarded chestnuts
grow out of the rubble like full, folded ferns.
Inside the nearby church, amonst fragments of statues and frescoes,
a monk shepherds a pig,
a cat lies curled on a cushion,
as an angel performs the annunciation to a Mary
who stands quietly beside an inkwell
equipped with two quill pens and a blank scroll of parchment.
Scarcely touched by the outside sunlight,
the angel dissolves in flakes of pink pigment,
a mixture of salmon and rose
tossed across chasms of painted thunder.
Outside again time is brilliant, sunlight mordant:

here everything is being etched away at the surface
by its own intense colour which the sun leads outwards.
So I take out a pen to collect all these fragments
before Montelupone shall crumble away
into a random confusion of indecipherable tesserae.
But, as I round a corner, a huge concrete-mixer,
blue like some monstrous organ welded from the sky,
pounds and thunders turning everything around me to watered
                                                    pumice.

Now, with these words more than half useless,
I drop quickly down again into the hot swimming plain
that bubbles greenly outwards,
steaming under the smell of warm bean-flowers,
to swirl and eddy, brim and boil over
into the white tides of the corrosive sun.

XI: At six o'clock

Walking at six o'clock in the evening
when the sun crawls down like a wise old crab
behind the farms and ilex trees,
and the valleys step
steeply down into their own green twilight,
I see the woman lift
water out of the well on the clover hillside,
up from the cool dark shaft,
till the liquid from the swinging pail
catches the last evening light and splashes
over her knees and thighs turning them dark,–
deep brown,
under the clover's moistly folding trefoil
and the blonde heads of the defeated grass.

33

XII: A White Goose

Stand casually:
look down into the deserted farmyard.
Only the white goose squares his awkward way across the paving,
leaving the black pronged marks of feet
until the pink wall stops his frozen head.
Alert, he turns,
his tiny snail-coiled eye
waiting for the night to fall,
the grass to turn to black,
the trees to curb his whiteness in the encaging yard.

XIII: Peasant-woman going home

Wrapped up in work and farm and landscape as by a rug,
she bleeds off weather only when she sleeps:
she speaks of summer in her heavy breath,
the creased sheets grumble with her turning thighs:
her green-stained fingers clutch the spring's deep root.
She lifts an elbow;
under it the moon
slides like a neighbour to be nursed by her.

Three Negatives

for R

I

On the Mountains above Garulla

Into distances
between here and Macerata
nothing moves, is blue.
While you, in the street down there, go thinking of hand-bags,
                                      shopping,
I, fifty kilometres away,
lie on the knee of this mountain looking down
through the blue
               modestly misted distances.

As behind me La Priora props
her great hip upward in the sun,
before me you, perhaps,
in the street down there, are glancing back to complain –
as the leaves flame dazzling above your upflung head, –
of "misleading distances."
Misleading distances? Perhaps . . .
Then where am I: and where are you?

I turn
to those further slopes above my head
where butterflies falter outwards, swallows fly
in long parabolas towards the hidden sea.
Far beyond you there the mist
still gardens the Adriatic.

Perhaps, at this moment too, you turn that way to see
that image from two days ago
of a faded green Madonna lost in a farmyard church.
There nests of pagan shadows crouched about her head
and that disused cloister just beyond
still stank with vats of cheese that shouldered back
black demi-johns of wine,

                     a rat or two, perhaps,
and a pregnant goat that bled.

Perhaps you, too, now turn to see
this mutual memory printed there,
like mist on mist
                before mist moves away.

II

Below Garulla

At three o'clock, I began to go down the hill.
It was intensely hot: I took off my shirt.
Bending forward, my arms above my head,
I saw openings of light through the shirt's grey mesh,
and below, two blue-trousered legs,
dusty shoes on a road leading downwards;
then, between my feet,
bright green like a pulped maize-leaf,
a dead lizard, smashed on the road,
its blood, like the seeds of a ripe fig,
uncurling from a pale green mouth.
I stood up,
dragged on my shirt again:
and it seemed that now everywhere
the white, sun-inflamed dust was pressing back
the lost colours that for thousands of years
had lain hidden inside everything.

III

In the Valley

A stream, deep in the valley,
inhabited only by an electric-blue dragonfly,
and my two bare feet
                    cold as stones.

A leaf passes,
a breeze blows behind me over a shelf of rock
and high above the tall alders and walnut-trees,
a kestrel goes calling anxiously
into the long hot afternoon.
Below, in the cleft of water,
my two feet die open
                    like pink fish-bones;
and the kestrel's image,
                    pitched in the water's nearer mirror,
gradually glides between tree-tops
                    fading into the erasing silver
of the sky's bright negative.

Two Views of Macerata

I

In the Public Gardens, Market Day: July '67

It was a hot day,
blood like great sacks
hanging in the loops of the hands as we sat
under the chestnut-trees, where the cicalas' rusty gasp
blocked the hot air: and above, in the town
the market filled up each gap between wall and hill's brink
with fruit, leather, fat, shoes, cheese,
all lying puddled in ink-filled shadows.
There, under the tiled arcade
like a hubbub of grandiloquent bees,
the contadini, up for the day on their hilltop of bargaining,
buzzed and swarmed, swelled and spat:
and we, down below in the public gardens,
lay watching the trees shake like love,
green on the blossoming sky;
watching the children sprawl
animal-like in the grass.

We lay there, part watching, part sleeping,
till the long hot afternoon
spread itself out round the town,
linking each valley-farm, each field, each vineyard, each roof,
with the spread of our hands and arms.
There we slept:
then the clock rang us back;
and we stared, half-awake, lids lifting from sleep,
as we watched the farmers stream off,
freshly arrogant in their best suits,
rich with the sunlight on pots, pans, purring Fiats,
and the warmth of their fat cheque-books
wrapped cosily round their full hearts.

Opposite Vico's House, Moon-Day: July '69

"Here lived de Vico" . . . so the inscription says:
and here across the street,
the students sit at café tables
discussing whether history has ever moved
in ascending spirals, as Vico once maintained,
or whether life declines
into a puffy plethora ringed round by gadgets, artefacts and kitsch.
Here, sipping mouthfuls of bibite,
curling tongues round spoons,
or licking fingers sweet with anisetto,
for them it seems, today
that historicity has settled back
into a passive beauty, sadly self-absorbed.

"The moon?" they say. "There's nothing there
but rocks and dust.
Not even gravity to make you want to walk
bare-foot. Go all that way
to find that dust is dust!
That spiral ended with a dullish thud.
Moon-flop!
Aspire . . . to that!"

Here, on this café's pavement,
drenched in light, now nothing really moves,
but blood and tongues and music
going nowhere. Here hands count off
the minutes gently, all sad millionaires of time
where no investment counts.
Here toes are stretched, and forearms scratched,
and hair is combed, and yawns extend to laughter,
– only laughter travels back
in a slow unwinding spiral down these throats.

Now as they sprawl at café tables
in the open palm of this benevolent sun,
the moon, so casually discussed, is soon forgotten.
The space they care to travel lies enclosed
within the confines of their senses' affluence.
And Vico's spiral?
Perhaps they'll find it spinning inwards:
a nerve's-length away is the longest trip they'll take.
'Al centro del corpo: andata e ritorno'.
– Can Vico's spiral keep on going down?

Auto Ritratti

I

The sun, the summer air,
now drifts through hair on nipples growing grey:
my moted eyes
stagger for distant trees and mountains,
but miss the nearer stones precise geography.
Only the gay olfactory nerve
swings into youth again to assess
the scent of running water, the press of hay and weeds and

ox-dung,

the bitter-sour of trout in streams,
of dogs in yards,
of hens awaiting death.
Till, turning my head,
the scent of sun-warmed flesh
is like a hunger without thirst.
My fingers touch the stream.
– Cool water coolly goes beyond these stones,
but sun dies hard like glass.

II

Bones,
in a little shell of muscle and warm skin,
why do you stand so cold,
one finger in the air?
The blood's undressed,
the heart lies down,
only the bones still stand and will not sleep,
– and dare not dream.

III

Miracles happened once, now less and less.
As one grows older
even an Italian landscape has that opaque look
too-often visited places wear.
Unless
some thunder suddenly flattens through the mountains,
this green valley large with summer's ease
remains a random green,
this blue scorched sky
remains at finger's end familiar as self's skin.
This water's talking drinks such blank success
I scarcely listen. If miracles came to pass
I'd barely see them now.
Yet storms are the frozen half of miracles:
their ice clings tight to skin until our dying hurts.
– Dying-and-hurting now's the most we get.

IV

Hung in the mountains under threads of clouds,
where kestrels slowly round the silence into one
long hissing of damp grass –
hoppers I melt
this stone-grey mountain in my bones:
till, straddling the ridge I face
grey space, blue openness
and the long shaking fall
to Adriatic distances. My face
cuts at the sea, my shoulders lean
back into boulders. So the earth turns on:
I, flattened like a fly against a spinning ball,
turn with it as it moves me carelessly
through frames of casual light.

Now light grows faster,
strips back at wrist and toe, falls free
as kestrel's falling,
under me cuts cloud from deepening mountain,
scoops out the valley's side and in the distance reads
the coast's cool argument against the insistent sea.
The sun grows warm, the white rocks burn:
I listen through the air
and the softly
                    pulsing
                            silence
throbs with emptiness.